The Secrets of URANUS

by Thomas K. Adamson

CAPSTONE PRESS
a capstone imprint

Capstone Press
1710 Roe Crest Drive, North Mankato, Minnesota 56003
www.capstonepub.com

Library of Congress Cataloging-in-Publication Data
Adamson, Thomas K.- author.
  The secrets of Uranus / by Thomas K. Adamson.
      pages cm. — (Smithsonian. Planets)
  Summary: "Discusses the planet Uranus, including observations by ancient cultures, current knowledge of Uranus,
and plans for future scientific research and space exploration"—Provided by publisher.
  Audience: Ages 8-10.
  Audience: Grades 2 to 4.
  ISBN 978-1-4914-5869-3 (library binding)
  ISBN 978-1-4914-5902-7 (paperback)
  ISBN 978-1-4914-5913-3 (eBook PDF)
1. Uranus (Planet)—Juvenile literature. I. Title.
  QB681.A329 2016
  523.47—dc23   2014046201

Editorial Credits
Elizabeth R. Johnson, editor; Tracy Davies McCabe and Kazuko Collins, designers;
Wanda Winch, media researcher; Tori Abraham, production specialist

Our very special thanks to Andrew K. Johnston, Geographer, Center for Earth and Planetary Studies, National Air and Space Museum,
Smithsonian Institution, for his curatorial review. Capstone would also like to thank Kealy Gordon, Smithsonian Institution Product
Development Manager, and the following at Smithsonian Enterprises: Ellen Nanney, Licensing Manager; Brigid Ferraro, Director of
Licensing; Carol LeBlanc, Senior Vice President, Consumer & Education Products; Chris Liedel, President.

Photo Credits
Black Cat Studios: Ron Miller, 15, 23; © Calvin J. Hamilton, 29; Capstone, 18; Corbis: NASA/Roger Ressmeyer, 27; Courtesy of Dr. Leigh
N. Fletcher, 16; Getty Images: Dorling Kindersley/Peter Bull, 11, Science Photo Library: Carlos Clarivan, 19, Universal Images Group, 17;
Granger, NYC, 9; Lunar and Planetary Institute, 5 (bottom), 14; NASA: ESA/A. Feild (STScI), 25, ESO, 24, JPL, 20 (bottom), JPL-Caltech,
cover, back cover, 1, 5 (back), 21 (top); Science Source: California Association for Research in Astronomy/W.M. Keck Observatory/Lawrence
Sromovsky, University of Wisconsin-Madison, 13, Wellcome Images, 8; Shutterstock: Stefano Garau, space background; Thinkstock:
Photos.com, 6, 7

Direct Quotations
Page 16 from Leigh Fletcher's blog "Planetary Wanderings," planetaryweather.blogspot.com

Printed and bound in the USA.
009889R

Table of Contents

A Boring Planet?

We didn't know much about the planet Uranus before Voyager 2 flew by it in 1986. The robotic spacecraft took the first close-up photos of the planet. No one was sure exactly how Uranus would look.

The first images looked boring. They showed no clouds, no storms, just a pale blue-green color. If Uranus had any interesting features, it was keeping them a secret.

But by the time Voyager 2 left Uranus, it had made some exciting discoveries. And since then, Uranus has revealed more surprises. Images from telescopes have shown a more interesting side to Uranus and its moons. Uranus was even hiding its own set of rings!

Uranus is about four times wider than Earth. If Earth were as wide as a dime, Uranus would be as wide as the top of a coffee mug.

Fast Facts

Distance from Sun: 1.8 billion miles
(2.9 billion kilometers)

Diameter: 31,518 miles (50,723 km)

Moons: at least 27

Rings: 13

Length of day: 17 hours

Length of year: 84 Earth years

Earth

Uranus

Discovering Uranus

Uranus can be seen with the naked eye, but it's very difficult. The night has to be clear and perfectly dark. And you have to know exactly where to look. Ancient cultures did not know anything about Uranus. It was not bright enough for them to notice. No one was able to track this planet before telescopes were invented.

Early astronomers using telescopes didn't think Uranus was a planet. William Herschel observed Uranus in 1781 with a telescope he built in England. When he saw Uranus as a fuzzy disk, he first thought it might be a comet.

Herschel

But a comet as bright as this object would have to be close to the Sun and moving quickly. The object Herschel saw was moving too slowly to be a comet. Based on this motion, Herschel knew it had to be farther away than Saturn. Something that bright and that far away had to be a planet. Uranus was the first planet to be discovered with a telescope.

Uranus was spotted 21 times before Herschel revealed its secret identity as a planet in 1781.

Herschel's telescope

King George III of England was impressed with the discovery. He gave William Herschel a job as Royal Astronomer. Herschel wanted to name the new planet Georgium Sidus, or "The Georgian Planet." Outside of England, no one liked this name.

Scientist Spotlight: William and Caroline Herschel

William Herschel was a musician who later became an astronomer. He and his sister Caroline built their own telescopes. They saw Uranus with their telescope on March 13, 1781. They observed it carefully for many nights. They realized that its orbit matched that of a planet and not a comet. After the discovery William went on to study nebulae. Caroline discovered eight comets. She was the first woman in recorded history to discover a comet.

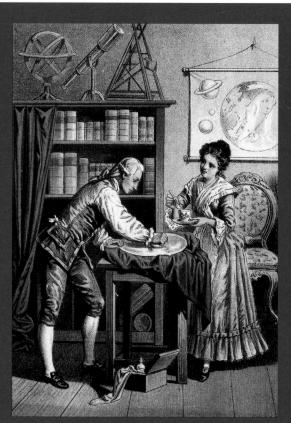

Many names were suggested for the newly discovered planet. Eventually German astronomer Johann Bode's suggestion of Uranus was chosen. The other planets are named after Roman gods, but Uranus was named after the Greek god of the sky.

What's Going on in the Atmosphere?

Like the other gas giant planets, Uranus has no solid surface. It has a thick atmosphere made of gases. Uranus is so far from the Sun that its gases are icy. So it's also called an ice giant planet.

Uranus' atmosphere is mostly made up of hydrogen and helium. It also has a small amount of icy methane. The methane gas causes the planet's pale blue-green color. Methane absorbs red light. That leaves green and blue to be reflected.

Moving from the atmosphere toward Uranus' core, the gases gradually become thicker. The gases turn into an icy slush. Deep inside the planet, temperatures could actually be very hot. Scientists are not sure if the planet has a solid or liquid core—it's still a secret!

Uranus appears to be one solid color. But its atmosphere actually has different bands and zones created by gases rising and falling. Astronomers enhance telescope images to see them.

Raining Diamonds?

In Uranus' upper atmosphere, methane may fall from clouds in raindrops the size of basketballs. As the drops fall deeper in toward the planet's interior, growing pressure squeezes the methane together. The pressure is so high that the carbon in the methane could turn into diamonds.

core

The first photos of Uranus didn't show the colorful cloud patterns that Jupiter and Saturn have. Recently, strong telescopes have shown clouds appearing and disappearing around Uranus. The clouds are probably methane ice lifted up high in the atmosphere. Astronomers have even seen storms. The pale planet really isn't as dull as it first appeared.

In telescope images one of Uranus' poles appears hazy. But the other side has stormy clouds that show up as bright spots. Astronomers are still investigating how these storms change with the planet's seasons.

The temperatures in Uranus' cloud tops are the coldest of the major planets at -357 degrees Fahrenheit (-216 °Celsius). Uranus' thick atmosphere seems to be hiding another secret. There is little temperature difference between the equator and the poles. Something below the clouds is probably spreading heat around. Scientists are not sure what that could be.

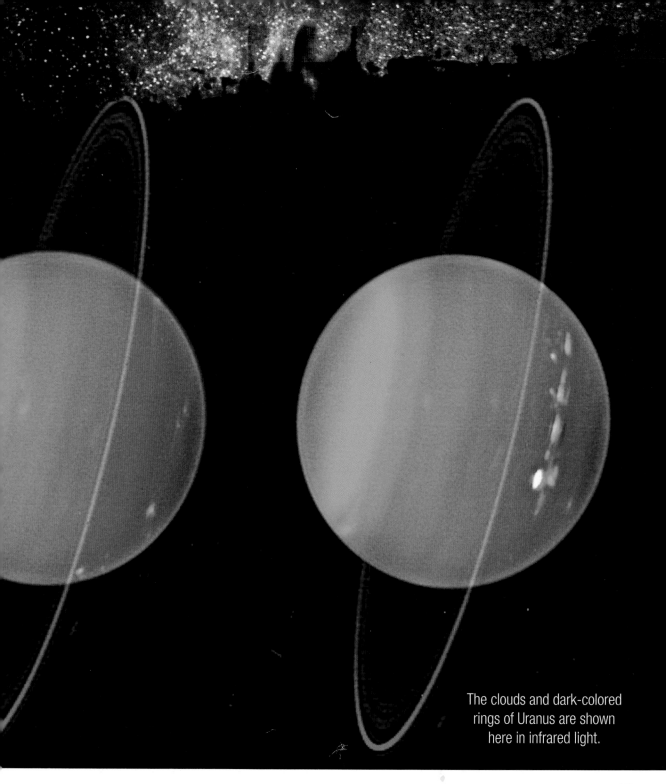

The clouds and dark-colored rings of Uranus are shown here in infrared light.

Spinning Sideways

Uranus is a fast spinner. The planet rotates once in just 17 hours. And it spins on its side.

Like all other planets, Uranus spins on its axis. But no other planet spins on its side. Uranus' axis is almost exactly flat relative to the ecliptic. Its poles actually point at the Sun during part of the year.

Gas Giant	Diameter
Jupiter	86,881 miles (139,821 km)
Saturn	72,367 miles (116,463 km)
Uranus	31,518 miles (50,723 km)
Neptune	30,599 miles (49,244 km)

Scientists think something huge crashed into Uranus early in its history. It could have been big enough to knock the planet on its side. It's also likely that the other giant planets caused Uranus' tilt. The giant planets are so huge their gravity could have affected Uranus.

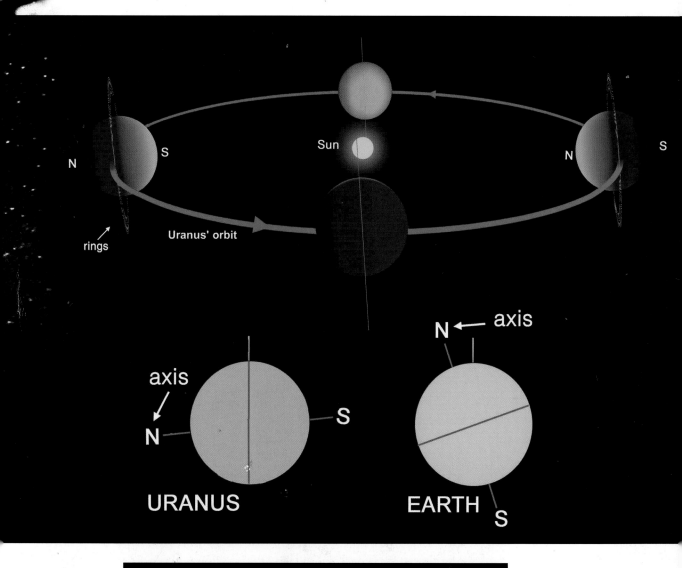

N

S

Sun

N

S

rings

Uranus' orbit

axis

N

S

URANUS

axis

N

N

S

EARTH

The ecliptic is an imaginary circle formed by the orbits of the planets. Think of it as a huge disk on which the planets move as they go around the Sun.

15

Twenty Years of Winter

Uranus' seasons are very different from Earth's. Each season lasts about 20 years. Because of the extreme tilt, Uranus' poles point at the Sun during summer and winter.

Scientist spotlight: Leigh Fletcher

Leigh Fletcher is a planetary scientist from England. Fletcher is an expert on gas giant and ice giant planets. He uses telescopes and information from spacecraft to study them. He even studies giant planets that orbit other stars. Fletcher says a new spacecraft needs to be sent to Uranus so we can reveal more of the planet's secrets. The gas giants can teach us about the beginning of our solar system, and even about planets around other stars.

"Exploration of Uranus and Neptune is a gaping hole in our current exploration of the solar system."
—Leigh Fletcher

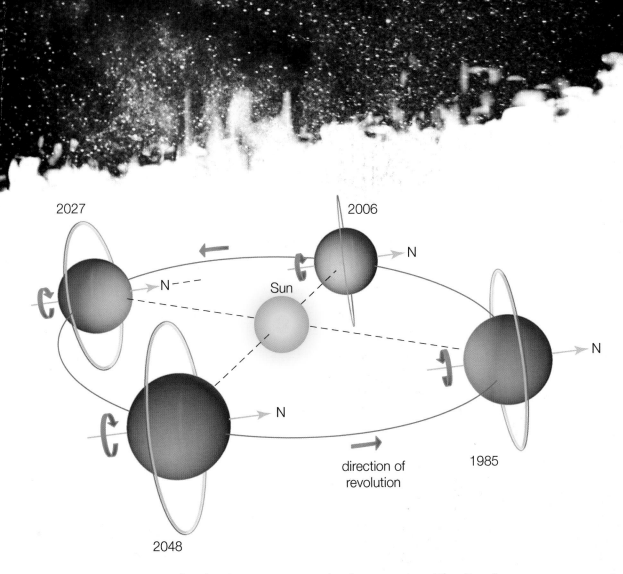

2027

2006

N

Sun

N

N

N

direction of
revolution

1985

2048

At one pole, the Sun never sets in the summer. The Sun just goes in a circle in the sky every 17 hours. At the other side of Uranus, the Sun never rises during this season.

As Uranus turns into spring and fall, its equator faces the Sun. As sunlight reaches some parts of the planet for the first time in many years, the atmosphere warms and huge storms erupt.

Voyager 2

It is not easy for a spacecraft to travel to the seventh planet. Uranus is 19 times farther from the Sun than Earth is. There is a huge amount of space between all of the giant planets. Even Saturn and Uranus, which are neighbors, never get closer than 944 million miles (1.52 billion km) to each other. That's almost 10 times the distance between Earth and the Sun.

Voyager 2 is the only spacecraft that has visited Uranus. It launched on August 20, 1977, and didn't get to Uranus until January 1986. After a journey of more than 8 years, Voyager 2 flew by Uranus. It took the best pictures we have of the planet and its large moons. Any new spacecraft to be sent to Uranus would probably take about the same amount of time.

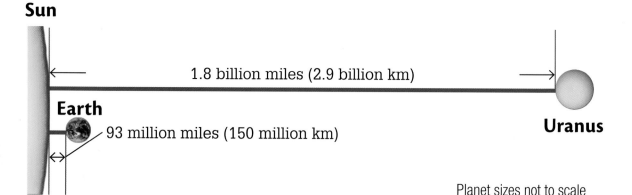

Sun

1.8 billion miles (2.9 billion km)

Earth

93 million miles (150 million km)

Uranus

Planet sizes not to scale

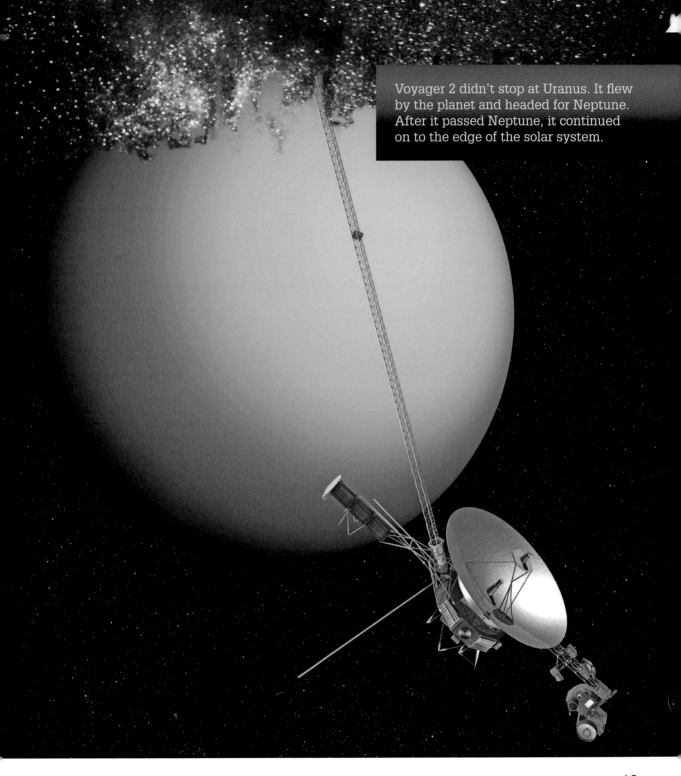

Voyager 2 didn't stop at Uranus. It flew by the planet and headed for Neptune. After it passed Neptune, it continued on to the edge of the solar system.

With no more planets to explore, Voyager 2 is now on its way out of the solar system. In about 40,000 years it will pass fairly close to the star called Ross 248. Between stars, "close" means 9.7 trillion miles (15.6 trillion km).

Voyager 2 has a large antenna. This 12.1-foot (3.7-meter) wide dish points toward Earth. It sends radio waves to Earth. Scientists read the information that the spacecraft records about the environments it explores.

Scientists are still in contact with Voyager 2 and collecting data from the spacecraft. They are learning more about what is in space that far from the Sun. Voyager 2 will likely run out of power by about 2025. Even without power the space probe will continue moving outward into the galaxy.

The Pulsar Map

Voyager 2 carries a map to our solar system. The landmarks on the map are a collection of stars that give off radio waves. These stars are called pulsars. By identifying the pulsars on the map, it would be possible for an intelligent life form to locate planet Earth in the Milky Way galaxy.

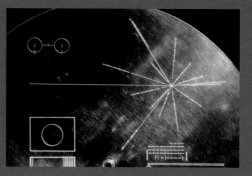

The alignment of the planets at the time of Voyager 2's journey allowed it to fly by all four giant planets.

Radio waves travel through space at the speed of light. That's 186,282 miles (299,792 km) per second!

Secret Rings

Uranus has 13 thin, dark rings. The rings are made up of dust, rocks, and boulders of ice. The rings were a secret for a long time. They were not discovered until 1977.

Uranus was about to cross in front of a distant star. Scientists wanted to observe this crossing to learn more about Uranus' atmosphere. Right before Uranus got to the star, the star's light flickered. It blinked again after Uranus passed in front of it. They soon realized it was the planet's rings passing in front of the star that caused the light to blink.

Voyager 2 discovered more rings in 1986. The Hubble Space Telescope found two more in 2005. All of the rings are less than about 6 miles (10 km) wide. The rings were possibly created by collisions between small moons.

The Hubble Space Telescope is a telescope that orbits our planet as a satellite. Because it doesn't have to "look" through our atmosphere, it can get better images of space and send them back to Earth.

Ring Plane Crossing

Scientists studied Uranus' rings in 2007 during a ring plane crossing. This special viewing opportunity happens when the edge of a planet's rings points directly at Earth and only a thin straight line is visible. Looking at the rings from the side, instead of above or below, allowed scientists to study how thick and dusty the rings are.

Still Finding Moons

Uranus has at least 27 moons. They are named after characters in stories by Shakespeare and Alexander Pope. Because Uranus is tilted on its side, the moons appear to move up and over the top of the planet instead of around the middle. But they all move around the planet's equator.

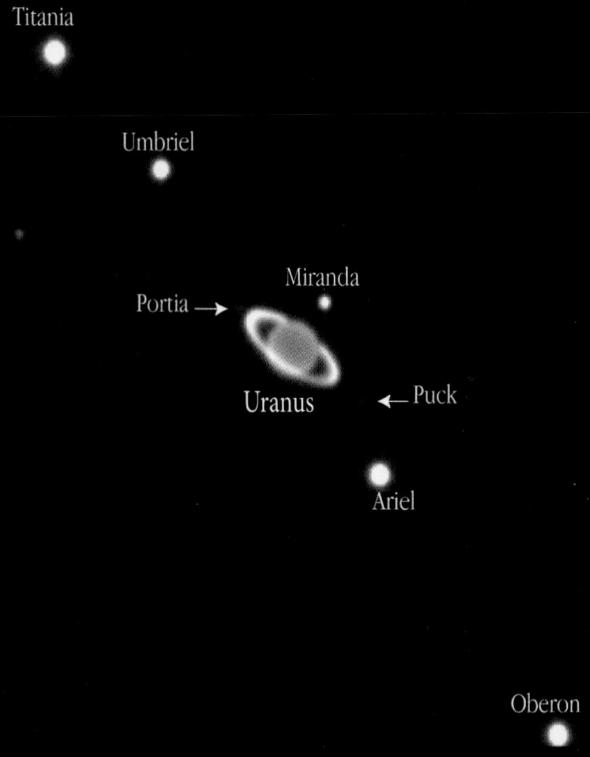

Titania

Umbriel

Portia →   Miranda

Uranus   ← Puck

Ariel

Oberon

Four outer moons move around Uranus in the opposite direction as the other moons. These moons might be small bodies that Uranus captured with its gravity.

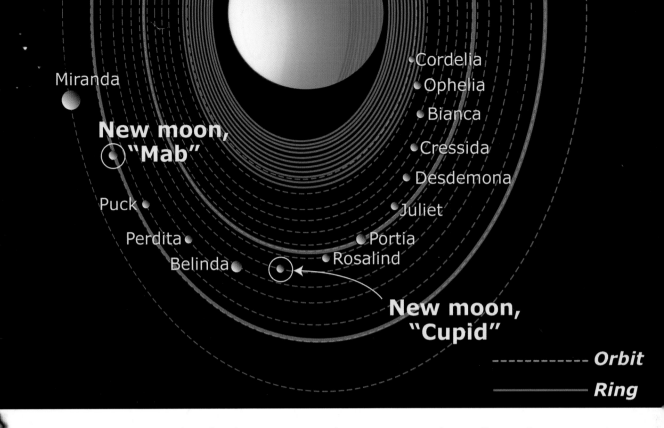

Miranda

New moon, "Mab"

Puck

Perdita

Belinda

Cordelia
Ophelia
Bianca
Cressida
Desdemona
Juliet
Portia
Rosalind

New moon, "Cupid"

- - - - - - - - - *Orbit*

————— *Ring*

Uranus has five large moons. The rest are much smaller and look dark and dirty. They are made of about half ice and half rock.

Titania is the biggest moon. It's about half the size of Earth's Moon. Oberon is the next biggest. Titania and Oberon have icy surfaces with lots of craters. Ariel is bright and smooth. Umbriel is dark but has a huge, bright round feature. It might be a crater covered with frost.

Voyager 2 also discovered several smaller moons. Telescopes, including Hubble, have discovered others. Some are really small and as black as asphalt. That's why they are so hard to find.

Two of Uranus' moons keep one of its rings together. They orbit on each side of the ring. They are called shepherd moons. Their gravity herds the dust in the ring into a line.

25

Miranda: The Strange Moon

Voyager 2 took close-up photos of Miranda. It passed close to this moon on its way to Neptune. Miranda surprised scientists. No one expected such a strange-looking moon.

The Voyager 2 photos showed deep ridges and canyons on Miranda. Bright and dark patches form odd shapes on its surface.

One possible explanation for Miranda's strange appearance is that something broke the moon apart and the pieces came back together. Now many scientists think that early in its history, rocky pieces of Miranda were pulled toward its center and icy pieces moved outward. But this process stopped, freezing it in this unusual position.

Miranda would have great scenery. One of its surface features is a canyon 12 times deeper than the Grand Canyon.

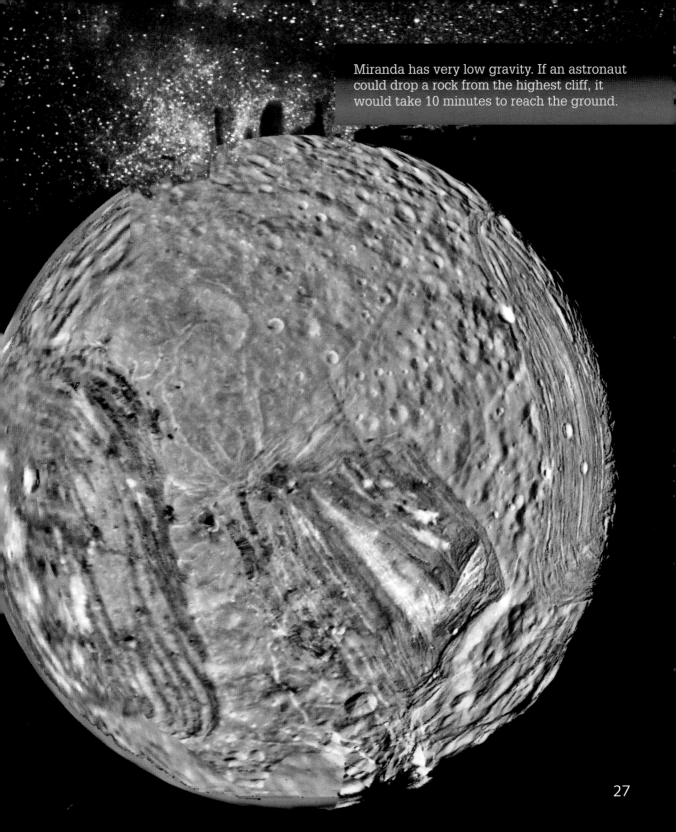

Miranda has very low gravity. If an astronaut could drop a rock from the highest cliff, it would take 10 minutes to reach the ground.

The Need to Discover

Astronomer Leigh Fletcher says we need to learn more about Uranus. He is part of a team working on a proposal for the European Space Agency to send a robotic spacecraft to Uranus. No spacecraft has ever orbited Uranus. Voyager 2 only flew by the planet. An orbiting spacecraft would provide much more information. We could learn more about how the clouds and storms change over the course of many years. Finding out more about the ice giants will help us learn more about how planets form.

When first photographed by Voyager 2 in 1986, Uranus appeared to be a gas giant without any interesting features. But recent discoveries reveal intriguing mysteries about this distant planet. How many more moons could it have moving around it? Can those moons give us clues about why the planet spins sideways? What would a new mission to Uranus discover?

Glossary

asteroid (AS-tuh-royd)—a small rocky body that orbits the Sun

astronomy (uh-STRAH-nuh-mee)—the study of stars, planets, and space

atmosphere (AT-muhss-fihr)—the mixture of gases that surrounds a planet or moon

axis (AK-siss)—an imaginary line through the middle of an object, around which that object spins

comet (KAH-mit)—a rock that goes around the Sun in a long, slow path; when close to the Sun, it has a long tail of light

crater (KRAY-tuhr)—a large hole in the ground caused by something such as a bomb or meteorite

ecliptic (ee-KLIP-tik)—the level that the planets orbit around the Sun; Uranus' axis is almost parallel to the ecliptic

equator (ee-KWAY-tuhr)—an imaginary line around the middle of a planet that is an equal distance from its north and south poles

gravity (GRAV-uh-tee)—the force that pulls things down or to the center of a planet and keeps them from floating away into space

Hubble Space Telescope (HUHB-uhl)—the telescope that orbits Earth in space; it allows scientists to study faraway objects in space, or other planets in the solar system

methane (METH-ane)—a colorless, odorless gas that can catch fire

nebula (NEB-yuh-luh)—a bright, cloudlike mass that can be seen in the night sky; nebulae are made up of stars or gases and dust

orbit (OR-bit)—the invisible path followed by an object circling a planet, the Sun, etc.

probe (PROHB)—a tool or device used to explore or examine something, as in a space probe

robot (ROH-bot)—a machine that is programmed to do jobs that are usually performed by a person

Read More

Chiger, Arielle, and Matthew Elkin. *20 Fun Facts about Gas Giants.* Fun Fact File: Space! New York: Gareth Stevens, 2015.

Owen, Ruth. Uranus. *Explore Outer Space.* New York: Windmill Books, 2014.

Taylor-Butler, Christine. *Planet Uranus.* A True Book. New York: Children's Press, 2014.

Internet Sites

FactHound offers a safe, fun way to find Internet sites related to this book. All of the sites on FactHound have been researched by our staff.

Here's all you do:

Visit *www.facthound.com*

Type in this code: 9781491458693

FactHound will fetch the best sites for you!

Super-cool stuff! Check out projects, games and lots more at www.capstonekids.com

Critical Thinking Using the Common Core

1. Read the text on pages 6 and 7. Why did Uranus go undiscovered for so long? What were the obstacles for identifying it as a planet? (Key Ideas and Details)

2. Read the text on pages 18 and 20, and look at the bar graph on page 18. Why has only one spacecraft traveled to Uranus? What might scientists have to think about when planning a new trip to Uranus? (Integration of Knowledge and Ideas)

Index